21

EDGE
BOOKS ™

GROSS

GROSS PRANKS

GUIDES

By Karen M. Leet

CAPSTONE PRESS
a capstone imprint

Edge Books are published by Capstone Press,
1710 Roe Crest Drive, North Mankato, Minnesota 56003
www.capstonepub.com

Library of Congress Cataloging-in-Publication Data
Leet, Karen M.
Gross pranks / by Karen M. Leet.
p. cm.—(Edge books: gross guides)
Summary: "Describes fun, gross prank ideas in a step-by-step format"—Provided
by publisher.
ISBN 978-1-4296-9922-8 (library binding)
ISBN 978-1-4765-1383-6 (ebook pdf)
1. Practical jokes—Juvenile literature. 2. Tricks—Juvenile literature. I. Title.
PN6231.P67L44 2013
818'.602—dc23   2012030972

Editorial Credits
Mandy Robbins, editor; Tracy McCabe, designer; Marcie Spence, media researcher;
Laura Manthe, production specialist

Photo Credits
Capstone Studio: Karon Dubke, 6 (background), 7 (top left), 10 (front), 12, 13 (middle
and bottom), 15 (bottom), 17 (middle and bottom), 24 (bottom), 25 (left), 29 (left);
iStockphotos: DonBrandenburg, cover (spider), Eratel, cover (design element),
jam4travel, 15 (middle), LuisPortugal, cover (design element); Shutterstock: aboikis,
6 (hand), Africa Studio, 28, Aksenova Natalya, cover (mouse), Andrew armyagov, 18
(background), Edoma, 9 (middle left), DonBrandenburg, design element, 20 (bottom),
Eky Studio, 1, 3, fatbob, 9 (bottom), 15 (top), Fotoline, 26 (bottom right), Garsya, 26
(bottom left), HamsterMan, 25 (middle), Ion Prodan, 26 (right), johnfoto18, 27 (top),
John Kasawa, 11 (right), K-i-T, cover (paint), Lane V. Erickson, 18 (bottom), Lazio, 9
(middle right), 14 (middle and right), Le Do, 18 (top), Levent Konuk, 8, linling, 17
(top), Marek R. Swadzba, 13 (top), Margaret M Stewart, 11 (left), 22 (right), mtkang,
20 (top), Myotis, 19 (bottom), Nataliya Hora, 29 (top right), NREY, 14 (left), Olena
Zaskochenko, 19 (top), photosync 22 (left), picsfive, cover (design element), 24 (top),
Potapov Alexander, 21, Raymond Kasprzak, 7 (top right), reborn55, 16 (bottom),
Sergey Furtaev, 4, Sergey Goruppa, 25 (right), Sofiaworld, 10 (background), South
12th Photography, 9 (top right), tacar, 16 (top), Ulkastudio, 29 (bottom right), Winai
Tepsuttinun, 27 (bottom), Yuri Arcurs, cover (woman)

Printed in the United States of America in Brainerd, Minnesota.
092012   006938BANGS13

Table of Contents

Pull Perfect Pranks

Do you get a good laugh from gross-out gags? Who doesn't? If you're a prankster whose motto is "the more disgusting, the better," this collection of pranks is for you.

Before you begin, check out a few tips to help you become the perfect prankster:

- Choose the right target. This is usually a friend or family member with a good sense of humor. Don't prank someone who might get angry or very upset.
- Don't do anything dangerous, destructive, or hurtful to anyone.
- When in doubt, try it out. Practice your prank ahead of time to get it just right.
- Choose the right time and place. Never pull pranks at school.
- Give it some drama, but don't overact. Practice your "Who me?" face.
- Don't let anyone else get blamed for your pranks, and clean up afterward if your prank made a mess.
- Stock up on prank supplies such as fake bugs and **severed** fingers.
- Spread out your pranks to keep them surprising.

 severed—cut off from the body

Here's a perfect prank for dog lovers. On a "disgusting scale" of one to 10, this prank is an 11. Enjoy this prank, but remember you'll have to clean up later.

POOP SCOOP

What you need:

a spoon, a bowl, peanut butter, powdered sugar, chocolate syrup

1 Mix a large scoop of peanut butter with powdered sugar until the mixture holds its shape nicely.

2 Stir in a few drops of chocolate syrup to get the best color.

3 Form the mixture into a poop-shaped log. If the mixture feels too sticky, add more powdered sugar.

4 Put the fake poop on an easy-to-clean floor or outside on the sidewalk.

5 Point out the "poop" to a friend, and offer to clean it up. Then pick it up, sniff it, and squish it through your fingers. You can tell your friend it's not real poop after he or she stops gagging.

POOP-THROWING CHAMPIONS: Some towns hold cow patty tossing contests. Competitors take turns tossing dried cow poop to see who can fling it the farthest. The best cow pie flingers make it all the way to the World Cow Chip Throwing Championship in Beaver, Oklahoma.

PUPPY PUDDLE

If you have an indoor dog, this is a fun prank to pull on your family. Make sure the puppy "pee" is on an easy-to-clean floor.

What you need:

water,
apple juice,
paper towel

1 Mix water with apple juice to get the right color.

2 Pour "pee" onto a washable floor.

3 Point out the "pee" puddle to your family. Grab a paper towel, and offer to clean up the mess. But instead of wiping the puddle up, stick a finger in it. Try not to laugh when your family gags.

REMEMBER TO CONFESS BEFORE THE DOG GETS IN TROUBLE!

Here's one more prank for pet lovers with indoor animals. The more red paint you use for your rodent "remains," the better.

MESSY MOUSE

1 Cut and tear fake fur into little pieces. Smear paint on the bits and let them dry.

2 Spread the pieces on an easy-to-clean floor.

3 Yell to your parents that your dog or cat has killed a mouse. Keep a straight face as they react with disgust.

What you need:
scissors, small piece of gray or light brown fake fur, washable red paint

CONFESS IMMEDIATELY, AND CLEAN UP THE MOUSEY MESS.

Do you really want to gross out a friend? Pack a picnic with an extra dose of **protein**. Add a real-looking fake bug to his lunch!

ROACHES

What you need:

picnic lunch including a sandwich, clear plastic sandwich bag, real-looking fake bug

1 Offer to make a picnic lunch for a friend.

2 Make a sandwich and put it inside a clear plastic bag.

3 Put the fake bug inside the bag.

4 Hand him the lunch, and wait for his reaction to the extra buggy protein.

on RYE

TIP: Get creative with this prank. You could even slip a fake bug into a meal your friend is already eating. Just make sure your friend doesn't actually eat the fake bug!

FACT People in many countries chow down on bugs. For example, moviegoers in Colombia snack on roasted ants instead of popcorn.

 protein—a chemical made by animal and plant cells to carry out various functions; protein is found in foods such as meat, cheese, eggs, and fish

SAMPLE MY PEE

Sharing is good—especially when it's nice, fresh "pee." The hardest part about this prank will be keeping a straight face.

What you need:

small bottle of apple juice, paper cup

1 Hide the apple juice and the paper cup in your bathroom.

2 Invite your friend over.

3 Go to the bathroom and fill the cup with apple juice. Flush the toilet so your friend thinks you really used it.

4 Come out with the cup of juice. Then tell your friend you heard that some people drink urine for health benefits.

5 Take a sip, and offer some to your friend.

FACT

Some people think drinking their own urine helps prevent or heal illnesses. Drinking urine is called "urophagia."

This prank is finger-licking good.
But please don't eat real dirt.
It can be full of nasty bacteria.

DELICIOUS DIRT

1 Put cookies into a plastic bag.

2 Crush the cookies with a spoon.

3 Moisten your fingers with water, and push them into the smashed cookies.

4 Pretend to come in from gardening or playing outside.

5 Tell your parents, "Wow, my hands got really dirty outside!"

6 Gross out your parents by licking off the "dirt."

What you need:

chocolate cookies, plastic bag, spoon

BLOODY PRINTS

Where did all that blood come from? Baffle your family with this bloody prank. Be sure to confess before they call 911.

What you need:

washable red paint, a bowl, washable green paint

1 Empty red paint into a bowl. Add a few drops of green paint to darken the red paint. Press your hands into the paint mixture.

2 Leave "bloody" handprints on the refrigerator door, in the sink, or on the bathroom cabinet.

3 Clean your hands, and wait for your family to freak out when they see the "bloody" prints.

CONFESS BEFORE SOMEONE FAINTS, AND CLEAN UP THE MESS.

Wear old clothes when you go on this trip. And be sure to "bleed" over an easy-to-clean surface.

BLOODY TRIP

What you need:

corn syrup, red food coloring, water, a bowl, a spoon, a sandwich bag

1 Mix 3 spoonfuls of corn syrup with 3 drops of red food coloring. Add a little water to thin the mixture.

2 Hide corn syrup "blood" in the sandwich bag in your hand. Don't seal the bag.

3 Walk to where your friends or family are. While you're walking, trip and fall to the floor.

4 Cover your nose with both hands, yelling as though you got hurt. Squeeze the fake blood between your fingers to "bleed" while you yell.

FINGER FOOD

This prank is great if your family enjoys chili. Who will still be able to eat after finding a finger in their food?

What you need:

chili, a fake severed finger washed with soap and water

1 On a day when your family is having chili for dinner, offer to help serve the meal.

2 Slip the fake finger into your victim's bowl. Wait for the reaction when your family member spots the finger!

FACT

In 2005 a Nevada woman sneaked a real severed finger into restaurant chili. She then tried to sue the restaurant.

This prank is a great use for hair left in combs and brushes. It will look like something creepy crawled into your target's dessert.

HAIR GELATIN

1 Make a hair ball out of loose hair from brushes and combs.

2 Offer to make dessert for your family.

3 Ask an adult to help you prepare the gelatin. You will make a prank dessert in one bowl and a real dessert in the other.

4 Add the hair ball to the lemon gelatin before the gelatin fully hardens.

5 Serve the gross gel, and wait for the disgusted reactions.

What you need:
loose hair, 1 package of lemon gelatin, 1 package of gelatin of any flavor, 2 bowls

DON'T LET ANYBODY EAT THE HAIRY GELATIN. THROW IT OUT AND SERVE THE OTHER BOWL INSTEAD.

SPLAT!

Swatting bugs can be delicious with this prank. Be sure to use a new fly swatter so you don't nibble real leftover bug bits.

What you need:

dark-chocolate-covered raisin, new fly swatter washed with soap and water

1 Be sure the table or counter surface is clean. Then put a dark-chocolate-covered raisin on it.

2 Have your fly swatter handy. When friends or family members walk in, swat the "bug."

3 Shock everyone by grabbing the "bug" and eating it.

Test your friends' and family's nerves. See who will panic over your fake bat.

BAT SCARE

1 Use the thread and eye screw to hang the bat in a dark corner. Have your friend hide somewhere, holding one end of the thread. Your friend can make the bat "dance."

2 Call your "victims," yelling that there is a bat in your house.

3 Act scared and excited as you point to the bat. Get your victims really worked up before confessing the truth.

What you need:

thread, eye screw, real-looking fake bat, a friend to help

SPIDER FREAK OUT

What you need:

a large fake spider, a friend to help

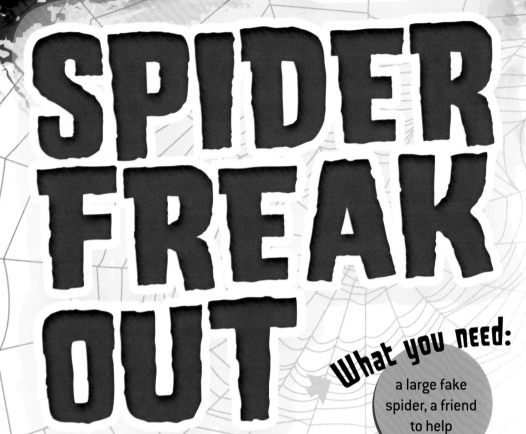

People who fear spiders suffer from arachnophobia. But anyone would hate having a spider in her hair. Watch a friend flip out with this prank, but choose your victim wisely. You don't want her to faint from fright.

1 While hiding the fake spider in your hand, yell, "There's a spider in your hair!"

2 Reach over and pretend to grab the spider from the victim's hair. Then yell something like "Gross!" and toss it to your other friend.

3 Continue tossing the spider back and forth with your friend, and watch your victim react.

4 Finally, drop the spider and let your victim in on the joke.

FACT Spiders can eat their own body weight in one meal. Then they can wait up to a year for the next meal.

BUGGY

You can use this prank if you need to return a shirt you borrowed from a friend. But beware—your friend may never lend you clothes again!

What you need:

strong glue,
fake bugs,
an old shirt,
a backpack

BOOGIE

1 Glue fake bugs all over the back of an old shirt—not your friend's actual shirt. Put it in a backpack.

2 Go to your friend and say something like, "Here's that shirt you loaned me."

3 Pull the shirt from the backpack, and yell for someone to get the bugs off.

4 Drop the shirt on the ground, and dance away from it. Meanwhile, watch your friend freak out.

BUG BITS: Did you know there are insect parts and rodent hairs in your food? These disgusting tidbits slip into our food supply during harvesting and processing. The U.S. Food and Drug Administration allows a certain number of insect fragments in our food. In cinnamon, for example, an average of 400 insect fragments per 1.7 ounces (50 grams) is allowed. In chocolate an average of 60 insect fragments per 3.5 ounces (100 g) is allowed.

The U.S. Department of Agriculture checks the food supply to keep it as clean as possible. Those insect bits or rodent hairs won't hurt us. But it's kind of disgusting to know they're there!

SNOT PLOT

What you need:

light corn syrup

Booger picking and wiping mucus on your sleeves is pretty gross. Imagine how disgusted your friends will be when you lick up your own snot after you sneeze!

1 First, wash your hands. Then hide a spoonful of light corn syrup in one of them.

2 Cover your nose with the hand holding the "snot" and pretend to sneeze.

3 Show everyone your slimed hand.

4 Lick the "snot" off your fingers.

mucus—a sticky or slimy fluid that coats and protects the inside of the nose, throat, lungs, and other parts of the body

Add some "maggots" to the ice cube tray. Next time you have guests over, use the tainted cubes to get everyone gagging.

MAGGOTS ON ICE

What you need:

an ice cube tray, water, short grain white rice

1 Fill the ice cube tray with water.

2 Add several grains of rice to each section of the ice cube tray and freeze it.

3 Once ice cubes are frozen, put them into your victim's drink.

4 Wait until your victim takes a sip, and then point out the "maggots" in the ice.

SHAMPOO SWITCHEROO

Eggs aren't just for breakfast anymore. Give your family members a shock in the shower, along with a healthy hair treatment.

1. Crack the eggs. Use the shells to carefully separate the yolks from the whites in two small bowls.

2. Throw out the yolks and pour the whites into the empty shampoo bottle.

3. Stand outside the bathroom and wait for your victim's reaction.

FACT

Egg whites are actually good for treating oily hair.

No one will expect this flavor in their sandwich cookies. Your friends may need a toothbrush after sinking their teeth into this minty treat.

TOOTHSOME TREAT

What you need:

a package of cream-filled chocolate cookies, a butter knife, white non-fluoride toothpaste

1 Take apart several sandwich cookies. Use the knife to scrape out the cream.

2 Replace the cream with white non-fluoride toothpaste.

3 Present the cookies to your friends. Give yourself one of the regular cream-filled cookies.

4 Take a bite, and wait for your friends to bite into the minty centers of their cookies. You might want to save some regular cookies as a peace offering!

ALREADY BEEN CHEWED

What you need:
a family trip to a restaurant, two pieces of gum

This prank is great for a family outing to a restaurant. It's a good way to kill time until your food comes.

1 After ordering your food, excuse yourself to the restroom. While there, chew both pieces of gum.

2 Hide the chewed gum in your hand until you get back to the table.

3 Reach under the table and pretend to find the gum stuck there.

4 Pop the gum into your mouth and start chewing, to the horror of your family.

Here's a prank for a food court outing. Pretend to dumpster dive for snacks!

TRASHED

What you need:
a plastic sandwich bag, a partly eaten sandwich, a partly eaten apple

1 Plan a mall food court outing with friends.

2 Fill a plastic bag with partly eaten food at home. Hide the bag in your pocket, purse, or backpack.

3 At the food court, lean over a trash can and pretend to hunt through it. (Don't actually touch the trash!) Sneak out the partly eaten food and show your friends your "find."

4 Offer to share your snacks from the trash. When your friends refuse, eat them up yourself.

Glossary

gelatin (JEL-uh-tuhn)—a clear substance used in making jelly, desserts, and glue

mucus (MYOO-kuhss)—a sticky or slimy fluid that coats and protects the inside of the nose, throat, lungs, and other parts of the body

protein (PROH-teen)—a chemical made by animal and plant cells to carry out various functions; protein is found in foods such as meat, cheese, eggs, and fish

severed (SEV-uhrd)—cut off from the body

Read More

Bell-Rehwoldt, Sheri. *The Kids' Guide to Pranks, Tricks, and Practical Jokes.* Kids' Guides. Mankato, Minn.: Capstone Press, 2009.

Hines Stephens, Sarah, and Bethany Mann. *Do It Now! Tricks.* Do It Now. San Francisco: Weldon Owen Inc., 2012.

Larsen, C.S. *Crust & Spray: Gross Stuff in Your Eyes, Ears, Nose, and Throat.* Gross Body Science. Minneapolis: Millbrook Press, 2010.

Internet Sites

FactHound offers a safe, fun way to find Internet sites related to this book. All of the sites on FactHound have been researched by our staff.

Here's all you do:

Visit *www.facthound.com*

Type in this code: 9781429699228

 Check out projects, games and lots more at **www.capstonekids.com**

Index